ACHIEVING FINANCIAL FREEDOM IN YOUR 30'S.

SERIES:
FINANCIAL FREEDOM AT ANY AGE.

ACHIEVING FINANCIAL FREEDOM IN YOUR 30's

Series "Financial Freedom at Any Age"
By: D.K. Hawkins
Version 1.1 ~November 2021
Published by D.K. Hawkins at KDP
Copyright ©2021 by D.K. Hawkins. All rights reserved.

No part of this publication may be reproduced, distributed or transmitted in any form or by any means including photocopying, recording or other electronic or mechanical methods or by any information storage or retrieval system without the prior written permission of the publishers, except in the case of very brief quotations embodied in critical reviews and certain other noncommercial uses permitted by copyright law.

All rights reserved, including the right of reproduction in whole or in part in any form.

All information in this book has been carefully researched and checked for factual accuracy. However, the author and publisher make no warranty, express or implied, that the information contained herein is appropriate for every individual, situation, or purpose and assume no responsibility for errors or omissions.

The reader assumes the risk and full responsibility for all actions. The author will not be held responsible for any loss or damage, whether consequential, incidental, special, or otherwise, that may result from the information presented in this book.

All images are free for use or purchased from stock photo sites or royalty-free for commercial use. I have relied on my own observations as well as many different sources for this book, and I have done my best to check facts and give credit where it is due. In the event that any material is used without proper permission, please contact me so that the oversight can be corrected

The information provided in this book is for informational purposes only and is not intended to be a source of advice or credit analysis with respect to the material presented. The information and/or documents contained in this book do not constitute legal or financial advice and should never be used without first consulting with a financial professional to determine what may be best for your individual needs.

The publisher and the author do not make any guarantee or other promise as to any results that may be obtained from using the content of this book. You should never make any investment decision without first consulting with your own financial advisor and conducting your own research and due diligence. To the maximum extent permitted by law, the publisher and the author disclaim any and all liability in the event any information, commentary, analysis, opinions, advice and/or recommendations contained in this book prove to be inaccurate, incomplete or unreliable, or result in any investment or other losses.

Content contained or made available through this book is not intended to and does not constitute legal advice or investment advice and no attorney-client relationship is formed. The publisher and the author are providing this book and its contents on an "as is" basis. Your use of the information in this book is at your own risk.

TABLE OF CONTENTS

TABLE OF CONTENTS 3

INTRODUCTION 5

CHAPTER 1 9

    The Courage to Achieve Financial Freedom. 9

CHAPTER 2 16

    Strategies for Achieving Financial Freedom in Your 30's. 16

CHAPTER 3 26

    How to Obtain Financial Freedom Through Internet Marketing. 26

CHAPTER 4 30

    Residual Income and Leverage to Achieve Financial Freedom. 30

CHAPTER 5 35

    Attain Financial Freedom and Earn Money Through Diverse Revenue Streams. 35

CHAPTER 6 45

    Using The Power Of Manifestation, You Can Now Manifest Your Desires And Achieve Financial Freedom. 45

CHAPTER 7 50

    What Does It Take to Begin Living the Life You Desire? 50

CHAPTER 8 56

Financial Planning For Individuals, Peace Of Mind And Freedom. 56

CONCLUSION. 61

INTRODUCTION.

It's possible to live a financially free life even if you don't work all the time, as long as you have enough money. Unless you were born a billionaire, financial freedom is probably not a concern for you - but it was undoubtedly for your billionaire parents.

For the vast majority of us, financial security is a daily aspiration. As such, here is how to obtain financial freedom and the two powerful rules to follow. You're undoubtedly already aware that the key to financial freedom is an investment. Investment is the equivalence of passive income.

Passive income is the same as financial security without actively working. This means more time to enjoy life while still having the financial wherewithal to do so. This entails waking up each day without concern for being late for work or performing arduous day jobs. This entails being able to meet financial obligations without working five or more days a week.

This indicates that your revenue has exceeded your expenses. We must work on it. We cannot just ask how to obtain financial freedom and expect everything to fall into place before our eyes. To see your aspirations come true, you must be willing to follow the rules.

Financial success is not for the faint of heart and involves introspection, perseverance, and commitment. To be clear, this is NOT a get-rich-quick program; it is about gaining financial freedom, whatever that means to you personally. It's about the road of achieving financial freedom through education and experience so that you can both preserve and generate financial freedom.

The first steps toward financial freedom begin with self-reflection. Self-reflection techniques assist you in comprehending your thoughts and behaviors; after all, your attitude and behavior determine your results. After all, who else will propel your objectives ahead and guide you down YOUR path to financial freedom?

There are "X stages to financial freedom." This is achievable if we were all constructed the same way, with thoughts, habits, personality, beliefs, and attitudes. The truth is that the number of steps required to reach YOUR financial goals is entirely dependent on YOU and your application of these tools and strategies.

Consider what you see in the mirror (or on your bank account). What you see reflects the financial results you've accomplished thus far! How does it appear? OK?

Could it be improved? What could be worse?

Whatever response you give will be contextualized concerning your environment and peers. Your definition of success will differ from those around you and throughout the world. As a result, we will concentrate on defining what financial freedom (or, more precisely, your financial freedom) means to you.

There is no point in playing the money game unless you have established your financial goals from the start; without goals, it is impossible to WIN. Self-reflection strategies assist you in comprehending your thoughts and behaviors; after all, your attitude and behavior determine your results.

A component of self-evaluation includes examining our fundamentals, our beliefs, and our attitudes toward money. Also, we will examine our habits, why we perform particular actions or duties automatically, and why our subconscious mind takes over automatically.

Unless and until you establish your financial goals, there is no purpose in playing the money game; without goals, it is impossible to WIN." We need to concentrate on and change some of our non-supportive behaviors that are detrimental to our financial well-being.

CHAPTER 1

The Courage to Achieve Financial Freedom.

I know that you have heard this many times before. You have tried to implement and to follow the advice of others and live this particular way as well. I know I did. Even if you didn't hear this particular saying from someone else, you may have assumed that "If I live this way, then I will have financial freedom. I thought this approach as well, and it backfired.

I'm referring to enjoying the easy life. The assumption is that the same problems you do not deal with will eventually go away. Or another way to think is that if I just had financial freedom, I would be better off.

The odd thing about this is that it keeps you from achieving more incredible wealth and financial independence. Why?

Because you may not have the bravery to achieve financial freedom and not even be aware of it.

Think about it.

When your greet the morning, you say, "I am so glad that I only have enough money just to get by," or "I just love looking at my bank account, which may include overdraft. while still not being able to pay all of my bills" or "I'm just looking forward to having more life left at the end of my money while feeling anxious and stressed out daily." No. Nobody anticipates this.

However, this is what is occurring, and, as bizarre as it may sound, it has to do with a lack of guts in pursuing financial freedom. So what am I getting at?

You will encounter an equal balance of support and difficulty, pleasure and suffering, praise and criticism wherever you are or whatever you do in life. Along with this, you'll have those who admire and despise you. in equal measure.

And the important component of this is the more wealth you have (combined with financial freedom), the more of each you will have in equal measure.

Consider the world's wealthiest individuals. What are your observations?

As an illustration, consider Donald Trump. You'll see that Trump has millions of detractors and millions of supporters. You'll witness millions of people accusing him of being a selfish jerk and millions praising him as a friendly and compassionate man.

Also, you may be unaware that the wealthiest individuals (including Trump) assume many risks, and it is precisely by taking these risks that they receive the benefits.

Most individuals believe that if they are affluent and have financial freedom, they will have a more effortless and happier life. The reality is that you will experience an equal amount of ease and struggle and the other pairs of opposites listed previously, and the more your financial wealth, the more of each you will receive.

If you seek more benefits, you should anticipate taking more significant risks. If you want a thousand people to support, praise, and like you, prepare for a thousand individuals to criticize, criticize and despise you. Pleasures and sorrows are on an equal footing, as are people's opinions of you as generous and greedy.

Now for what most people subconsciously believe.

"If I am wealthy (in the millions) and financially independent, people will believe I am filthy rich. I don't want people to think that way about me. People who formerly liked me and even those I don't know will no longer like me. Due to my financial success, I am now subjected to increased criticism. They're putting me to the test more.

Suddenly, folks, I don't know and haven't heard from in years may approach me and ask for money. If I say "no," they would despise me and believe I am stingy and greedy. I thought life would be simple, but now there are more accountability and obligations, and it appears as though I'm constantly under the microscope in the eyes of many others.

I'm not interested in any of this and will do anything to avoid having to deal with it."

This is precisely what occurs when you believe you will be better off due to more money and financial freedom. Of course, you can do something to prepare for the possibility that this will not occur, allowing you to live a financially independent existence.

But first and foremost, you must have the fortitude to do so.

Do you possess the fortitude to embrace both opposition and support equally?

Do you have the fortitude to deal with the same number of individuals who dislike and like you?

Are you courageous enough to deal with those who are repulsed by your presence? As well as those who are sincere and smile at you?

Do you have the fortitude to let go of certain people in your life while allowing others to enter?

Do you have the fortitude to be perceived as selfish while simultaneously being known for your generosity and compassion?

Do you have the fortitude to be viewed as "filthy rich" and "fortunate" in the same way someone who has earned their way and adds significant value to others does?

Do you now have the fortitude to acknowledge that your life contains both difficulties and ease?

If you've responded affirmatively seven times, Congratulations since you now possess the bravery necessary to achieve financial freedom.

Utilize these principles to learn how to make the most of your existing circumstances to reach financial freedom.

CHAPTER 2

Strategies for Achieving Financial Freedom in Your 30's.

Most people in their thirties are on the lookout for novel ways to acquire financial freedom. People strive to improve their lifestyles and plan for the future. They desire more time with their families and less time working.

They want to live the life of their dreams but regrettably, most people never do, not because they don't want to or are lazy but because they don't know-how. Before I list the latest financial freedom concepts, let's look at what most people are doing in life today that is unlikely to result in financial freedom.

Let's examine some ideas that do not work:

1. Financial savings

While it is true that saving money can help you become wealthy and financially independent, the reality is that this process takes many, many years.

Now, I am not arguing that you should not save money; if you study successful individuals and principles, you will discover that saving money is one of the routes to prosperity. That is to say, saving money on its own is unlikely to be sufficient to achieve financial freedom.

There are a few explanations for this. First, most people squander their income; they do not have money left each month to save. Second, because inflation is typically larger than the interest rates offered by banks, you will ultimately lose money. As a result, I would not consider conserving money one of the newest ideas for financial freedom.

2. Work as an employee

The primary disadvantage of being an employee is that you exchange time for money. At the end of the day, we all have twenty-four hours each and every day (caught in the Rat Race). A small number of employees earn enough money to save/invest more than they spend. These individuals, on the other hand, are not typical. They are individuals who hold three or four degrees and were perpetual 'A' students.

These are truly intelligent men. Also, another significant disadvantage of being an employee is that you are not compensated fairly; you cannot be compensated fairly because your employer must benefit from you.

3. Self Employed

Having your own business is preferable to working for someone else since you are in charge of your own schedule and destiny. Self-employment has the significant drawback of requiring you to trade your time for money.

If you do not work, you will not be compensated. The strategies outlined above are not regarded as cutting-edge ideas for financial freedom and are unlikely to result in financial freedom because they all lack leverage.

Let's examine some of the most recent ideas for achieving the financial freedom that works:

1. Begin your own business from the ground up:

You may be able to start your own business if you are enthusiastic about a particular product or service or if you have identified unmet market demand potentially because you'd have to do a lot of homework before investing. Most multi-billion-pound firms were founded by a single person with an idea, often in a garage or spare bedroom.

If you recognize an opportunity and have the faith and determination to pursue it, you can achieve greatness! Microsoft, Virgin, Dell, and eBay are just a few examples of such companies. So, do you have the latest and greatest ideas for achieving financial freedom?

2. Multilevel Marketing / MLM

Starting a business from the start can be intimidating and pricey if you have no prior business expertise. This is where network marketing excels. You invest in a well-established system at a very cheap start-up cost and earn while you study. Network marketing is not comparable to traditional employment. If you work your firm correctly, you can grow it to a million-pound/dollar enterprise.

Likewise, if you do not work at it, you will fail. Unfortunately, network marketing is one of the newest ideas for financial freedom that people are skeptical about; they dismiss it as a pyramid scheme without understanding the distinction.

3. Real Estate Investing

Property investment is not a new concept for achieving financial freedom, having existed for centuries. Still, it is, in my opinion, the best medium to the long-term investment you can make.

According to statistics, property values in the United Kingdom have climbed by approximately 10% each year for the last 80 years. While property values have declined, they always recoup that loss and continue to appreciate it over time.

4. Stock Investing

You can purchase different shares, including preference shares, bonds, and gilts, but the most common is the ordinary share; ordinary shares merely represent a company's ownership.

Thus, when you purchase shares, commonly referred to as equities or stocks, you become an actual co-owner of the corporation. If ABC Plc, for example, has 100,000 shares worth $1 apiece and you purchase $1,000 worth of shares, you own 1% of the company.

It is important to remember that as an investor, you have a say in the business's operations by casting a vote at shareholder meetings. You also stand to gain financially if the firm is successful. If the firm performs well, the value of your investment should increase; however, if the same company performs poorly, then the value of your shares may decline.

5. Personal Development

The only way to become wealthy quickly is to win the lottery, inherit a fortune or steal a bank. The odds of winning the lottery are nearly nil, few people have wealthy grandparents, and the thought of prison does not appeal to the typical person. It is conceivable for each of us to earn millions upon millions of dollars each year, but the reality is that we have no idea how.

You will not find a book that contains a ready-made recipe for money that would instantly make you wealthy since if such a book existed, we would all be rich, wouldn't we? However, we must learn from the greatest.

If you see someone that is killing it at anything in life, learn from them, and surround yourself with their presence, knowledge, and experiences by reading and listening to audio training materials. Self-growth is the most undervalued of the latest ideas for financial freedom, although it is probably the most important.

6. Eliminate Bad Debts

First, we must recognize that there are 'good' and 'bad' loans and their distinction. Not all debts are considered 'bad.' Certain debts can generate revenue.

Today, the world's wealthiest people are in debt to the tune of millions of dollars, owing to their understanding of leverage. If you have a mortgage on the buy-to-let property and your tenants are paying it off, this is a 'positive' debt because it generates revenue. You wish to amass as much 'good' debt as possible.

Credit cards, car payments, and department store cards are all examples of 'bad debts. You are typically paying a fortune (up to 30%) for these debts, which just serve to restrict your monthly cash flow.

Create a structure to help you pay off these debts more quickly and be diligent about not getting into these problems again. This does not imply you will never own a fancy car or boat; instead, it means that if you spend wisely and expand your company correctly, you will be able to purchase that automobile outright.

7. Earn Cash Online

There are many different methods to earn money online while working from home, and one of them is through affiliate marketing. Affiliate marketing is the process of effectively advertising a website and being compensated for each visitor, subscriber, customer, and/or sale generated as a result of your efforts. Another method of earning money online is to start your website.

A web page on its own will not earn you money, but if you can build a website with a high volume of traffic, you can earn money by selling advertising space on your site.

Ebay is another method that has grown in popularity among people who work from home. Some people spend their days poring around eBay, looking for bargains. They purchase these products and resale them for a profit. Specific individuals create or distribute things on eBay, and they earn any money.

8. Create a one-of-a-kind product, service, or invention

Another approach to earning much money is creating an object or service that will simplify people's lives or desire many people. Inventing is far more complicated than it sounds, yet not all inventions must be intricate. I came upon a website selling plastic wishbones while exploring the internet.

Yes, someone has come up with a way to reproduce turkey wishbones for Thanksgiving in the United States; the concept is that you purchase a couple of them, and everyone at the table can have their wish granted, not just one. The company is now generating over 30,000 wishbones per year at a profit of $3 per bone.

CHAPTER 3

How to Obtain Financial Freedom Through Internet Marketing.

Financial freedom refers to an individual's ability to maintain his or her existing standard of living without working long hours or relying on others to cover expenses. In essence, a person must have a bigger monthly cash inflow than monthly cash outflow for living expenses.

Most of us aspire to financial freedom or too early retirement to enjoy life. This does not have to be a distant fantasy. Any individual who is capable of generating cash consistently and maintaining financial discipline can achieve monetary freedom.

Online marketing is a fantastic approach to earning cheap money from home. Making money online is so simple that anyone with spare time may earn extra money by focusing on the fundamentals of online marketing.

The Internet is the world's largest marketplace, offering many options to earn money and achieve financial freedom. This chapter discusses the most fundamental strategies for earning quick money using internet marketing.

Understand Your Possibilities.

Consider the various methods by which you could generate money online. Many efficient Internet marketing strategies might assist you in earning money online. SEO, blogging, advertising, article writing, building and managing online directories, affiliate marketing, and e-commerce are just a few examples.

There are many ways to generate money on the Internet today. Making money online may appear challenging if you are a beginner. However, the secret to online marketing success is to narrow your attention to a few concepts mentioned above rather than pursue every potential channel. Financial freedom does not happen overnight; you must work extremely hard to make it happen.

Possible dangers:

Many hazards are inherent in an online marketing business plan. Individuals may have higher costs than income, ineffective SEO, a lack of effective marketing initiatives, or an unproductive business strategy.

It is essential to consider all these hazards because you will be spending a significant amount of time and effort on this work, and thus it is essential to analyze the risks involved with it.

Utilize All Available Techniques.

When beginning an online marketing campaign, the most important phase is keyword research. After conducting adequate keyword research, you may start building links, increasing page rank, and utilizing different internet marketing strategies. These internet marketing strategies could include social networking, email marketing, and blog bookmarking. The aim is to develop a sound business plan and adhere to it while always attempting to improvise.

An online marketer cannot possibly employ all accessible marketing tactics. However, the greatest course of action would be to understand how the online market trends evolve thoroughly.

Also, remember to create an online business on ethical principles to ensure that your clients have complete trust in your organization and its products or services.

CHAPTER 4

Residual Income and Leverage to Achieve Financial Freedom.

What is residual income? What is leverage?.

Why do you require both to achieve financial freedom?

You may have heard these questions previously and received different responses. I'm here to set the truth straight, as these issues significantly impact my life.

Too often, financial freedom is equated with great riches. It is widely believed that the average person cannot achieve financial freedom unless they win the lottery or the jackpot. That is categorically untrue.

Indeed, financial freedom is defined as having sufficient "passive" or "residual" income to pay for one's living needs. I'm not talking about driving a $100,000 automobile and spending two months on vacation in Fiji. I'm referring to your life as it currently exists. Consider a person who earns $50,000 per year.

They could certainly get by on $40,000 per year covering their basic needs (housing, utilities, food, and transportation). The individual would only need a passive income of $40,000 per year to achieve financial freedom in such a case.

These results in the most important thing we can acquire in life. TIME FREEDOM! When you no longer have to trade your time for money to do what you want or feel called to do, you can live your life to the fullest.

LEVERAGE.

You are almost certainly being leveraged. I am and nearly everyone I know. My cousin's large firm leverages her time and talents for their benefit; the many affiliate programs in which I participate leverage me and my marketing for their benefit, and you are almost certainly being leveraged as well.

Having previously owned a residential home painting business, I profited each week using my employees' labor and talents. Thus, the question is not who leverages you butt who leverages you? If you are not utilizing leverage to achieve financial freedom, I wish you good luck with the lotto.

RETENTION OF RESIDUAL INCOME.

Someone once inquired whether I was a real estate agent who worked diligently to sell a home.

Which would I prefer: to collect my $5000 commission OR to receive $5 every time the front door opens and closes for the remainder of my years?

Although I responded immediately (and incorrectly) that I would prefer the entire commission upfront, the question lingered with me. After all, I was twenty years old at the time, and $5000 sounded like a fortune. I calculated the numbers both mentally and on paper. I ran the situation by a couple of friends. I still arrived at the same conclusion.

The numbers were correct; nonetheless, my perspective was limited. It wasn't until a family friend (a very successful insurance professional) asked me, "What if you sold an average of two houses each month for the next four years?" that my perspective shifted. That's 96 dwellings.

If the low-end average of opens/closes per home is five per day, that's a daily cost of $2400. , such a remuneration plan does not exist in real estate today (at least not that I am aware of), or else we would all be real estate agents. This is why many people seeking actual financial freedom gravitate toward the affiliate or network marketing industries.

To put it, residual income is money that is paid repeatedly for a single deed. Your insurance agent sold you your policy once but is compensated each time you pay your renewal premium to maintain your policy.

The affiliate or network marketing industries are the most pleasing possibilities to build a low-risk, low-cost business that leverages the power of leverage and benefits from residual income. Also, the days of viewing your friends and family as prospects and pestering them every time you see them are passed, owing to the internet.

Utilizing the internet to establish and grow a network marketing business is a beautiful idea! If done correctly, highly focused prospects will seek you out, rather than having to promote your firm to everyone you encounter constantly.

I made a long-term pledge that I would never own or operate another firm that did not leverage the power of leverage and provide the benefits of residual revenue. This philosophical shift has had a profound effect on my family. My cousin and I both work part-time, and I work from home. True financial freedom is on the horizon.

CHAPTER 5

Attain Financial Freedom and Earn Money Through Diverse Revenue Streams.

This chapter is intended to educate you on the various ways and means of earning money to achieve financial freedom through many sources of income.

This is not about receiving tips and advice on becoming an instant billionaire overnight or how to make easy and fast money; instead, this is about learning is proven and tested strategies for building lifetime many streams of income and becoming less dependent on a single job.

In summary of this discussion, these are the various sources of income available to enable anyone to earn money and earn a livelihood.

Sources.

* Primary - This is the most frequent type of income your employer provides in the form of a salary or wage and benefits in exchange for your work for the employer. Here, you earn money solely by working for your employer.

* Alternative - This is revenue generated through means or sources other than traditional office work or employment. Many people earn money by blogging, investing, selling on eBay, or starting an online business.

Types.

* Earned or Active - You earn money through working. You cease to make money when you cease to spend time performing the work that generates your income.

* Passive or Residual - Money works for you! In contrast to earned or active income, income

generation continues even when you are no longer working.

Given the two sorts of income, it's prudent to diversify your revenue streams and consciously shift toward residual or passive income creation.

What Qualifies as Passive and Residual Income for Everyone?

Having many sources of income is crucial for financial freedom. This significantly boosts your overall income and accelerates the growth of monetary riches. This will allow you to become less dependent on your principal source of income, which is currently your work, and eventually replace it entirely to attain financial freedom.

Thus, diversifying one's sources of income is essential for everyone nowadays, and this is made even more transparent by the following reasons:

* If you lose your job, your income does not "vanish," but rather "diminishes" because you

continue to earn money and generate cash through your many passive streams of income.

*Getting promoted in a company makes finding a job that pays the same as your previous one extremely difficult.

* Having multiple streams of income expedites your path to financial freedom. After all, the true test of financial freedom is when you are no longer reliant on your employment to cover your living expenditures.

* Having multiple streams of income enables you to utilize your resources and increase your flexibility. When you are not reliant on your employment for survival, you are in a much better position.

With few exceptions, the concept of fixed-paying regular work is dead; relying on a single source of income is extremely difficult, as many businesses do not dally in reducing labor for cost-cutting initiatives. I believe it is crucial for everyone to diversify their sources of income to mitigate income risk.

You spent a significant amount of money, effort, and time to get to your current position. Most employers require college graduation, while some require additional training and education.

Four years of college education consumed a significant amount of your money, effort, and time! Spending 15 minutes per week to develop many streams of income that provide at least $1,000.00 per month is not unreasonable!

Once you've established a stream of income (recurrent and passive), you can explore another one. In contrast, the one you've already established continues to create money and generate revenue for you, thus the passive concept.

To illustrate, if you have a source of income that provides you with at least $10,000 per month, you will continue to earn at least that much as income generation increases, even if you do nothing; this is the passive principle. In comparison, when you stop reporting to work at your office job, you stop earning money because you stop receiving your regular compensation.

Essential Values for Business Success in Multiple Streams of Income.

As previously said, we do not believe in get-rich-quick schemes and would want to warn you about various phony schemes that promise such deceitful schemes. We recommend that if you genuinely want to earn money and achieve financial freedom through many streams of income, you must keep the following values in mind:

1. Passion - Pursue activities that you truly enjoy and are passionate about.

2. Skill - Dedicate yourself to honing your abilities and developing into an expert.

3. Perseverance - Never anticipate immediate results. Be patient and persistent until you reach some

measure of accomplishment and continue to persevere to achieve even greater success.

4. Adaptability - Some tasks will require more effort than others to accomplish.

5. Determination - While other ideas may work, many do not; keep trying and do not become discouraged. Be persistent until you discover the marketing tool that works best for you.

6. Expand - Do not be satisfied with your initial success; seek more revenue streams to supplement your income and spread your income-generating capacity.

7. Incremental - Income gained from many sources adds up to a sizable portion of total income.

Become a Part-Time Entrepreneur.

As previously said, it is very dangerous to rely only on your current employment for money. As a result, being a part-time businessman is a prudent solution.

As a part-time company owner, you can retain your full-time employment and benefits while exploring new chances to develop and diversify your revenue streams. As a part-time company owner, you choose your schedule and work at your own pace to create many sources of income and earn money to reach financial freedom.

How to Begin.

The following are a few simple but essential steps to get you started with many streams of income:

1. Begin with the activities you enjoy. The rationale is for you to abstain from activities that you genuinely despise and dislike. Because you'll be committing time to your business, you should focus only on what you're enthusiastic about.

2. Create a detailed business plan. Conduct research and create an effective business plan. You'd

certainly want to enter into a viable firm and enables you to reach financial freedom.

3. Implement and complete. Without the execution and implementation of your company strategy, grand ambitions never become realities. This requires considerable courage and dedication to obtain the outcome you've always desired.

4. Constantly strive to improve. Not everyone succeeds with their initial business venture. Make a point of learning from your past failures and rely on collective expertise to attain success.

Where Do You Spend Your Additional Income?

Many alternatives become available to you whenever additional money begins to trickle in as you pursue financial freedom. Here are a few examples:

1. Pay off debts.

2. Establish an emergency fund.

3. Invest in different types of businesses.

4. Invest in additional multiple-stream income possibilities to diversify your revenue.

5. Conduct research and create your revenue stream.

6. Spend the money and live life to the fullest.

7. Contribute to charity and other deserving organizations with your financial assistance.

CHAPTER 6

Using The Power Of Manifestation, You Can Now Manifest Your Desires And Achieve Financial Freedom.

According to university studies, previous generations and even today's students focus a large portion of their courses on earning good grades and ensuring a bright future.

Is it true that your school taught you how to obtain financial freedom and live a life of prosperity and happiness through the power of manifestation?

While good grades are undoubtedly significant since they demonstrate dedication to life goals and objectives, I'm sure many of you were brainwashed by your teachers when you were students.

Your perception of an intensive future most certainly leads you to choose a career as a lawyer, medical professional, engineer, businessperson, or other occupation that guarantees a high income.

Your school did an excellent job assisting you in accomplishing your goals.

Is your school preparing you to manage your financial resources once your income and obligations begin to arrive?

Is your education preparing you to achieve monetary and financial freedom?

Your high-wage employment enables you to live in a large home, drive a fine car or truck, perhaps a sports motorcycle or a lake boat, join a country club, take yearly vacations and acquire the items you've desired.

Wait! Have you ever allowed worries of losing your profession or work to infiltrate your mind successfully?

Financial bubble deflated.

- Organizations relocate or may dissolve or downsize.

- Your business's cash flow statement continues to deteriorate.

- Perhaps the company's directors seek to reduce expenses.

They opt to lay-off employees who have been earning substantial weekly wages, and perhaps you are one of them, and your world comes crashing down.

A third and second mortgage secures your lovely lakefront home with a regional bank, and you've been dipping into your funds for the first few months to appease your lenders.

Quite soon, your lenders will continue to send you certified mail with notices of the impending foreclosure and will flood your voice mail with calls hounding you about your obligations.

I have covered the importance of actively creating the life you desire from within and reflecting it in the material world. As important as achieving financial success and attracting money is, managing your financial resources is important to living the life you desire and have always dreamed of.

Once you achieve financial security and are breathing normally, you will be able to exit the rat race. Then you shall have more free time to do the things you genuinely enjoy, such as exploring the world and living the life you truly desire!

Begin by learning how to obtain financial freedom.

Teach your children the value of the knowledge you are gaining in these new age times about manifesting your wishes, creating the life you desire, and comprehending how the law of manifestation genuinely works. In today's world, there is no shortage of resources available to you at your fingertips to educate, study, and grow with today's internet.

While money can be a double-edged sword that can either make or ruin you, by applying the universe's laws of attraction, they will be on your side if you can develop the ability to achieve financial freedom.

- Begin your journey toward financial freedom.

- Become educated.

- Be economically advantageous.

It's a good idea to gain a better grasp of obtaining financial freedom and educate yourself on accomplishing your goals and objectives to live the life you choose.

Begin a new adventure with the law of attraction steps that will guide you to achieving what you truly desire in this world.

CHAPTER 7

What Does It Take to Begin Living the Life You Desire?

Many people in their thirties feel that to obtain financial freedom, one must have a degree or be a genius, but this could not be further from reality!

Okay, so you're saying that money is required to make money, correct?

Not always. Indeed, some activities require no money at all; it all depends on what you want to do and how quickly you anticipate arriving. To begin, you must ascertain what you desire.

For instance, do you want to earn extra money to spend on trips, or do you want to earn a mind-blowing sum of money that will change your entire lifestyle?

Do you want to be able to pay off all your debt, cover your child's tuition, or do you just want to buy a boat and go sailing around the world?

Or do you desire financial freedom and all the perks that come with it?

It's entirely up to you in terms of size.

Nobody else has the authority to write your story but YOU. We should say it again since it's so impactful. There is only one person who has the power to write your story for you: YOU. No one else has the authority to write your story but YOU.

I will inform you that no one else has the authority to influence your story without your consent; without your permission, it will never happen. If this is something you wish to leave behind, I can attest from experience that it is difficult, but this transformation or shift is attainable, and the release from it alone is decisive.

It is a shift in your mindset and way of thinking. DARE to dream, DARE to BELIEVE in your dream, and you are well on your way to achieving it. This belief will expand your potential for creativity and assist you in achieving your personal goals.

Second, make a note of it. On a scrap piece of paper, jot down the first five aspects of your life that you desire. NOTE: Try to keep this as positive as possible; avoid mentioning any drawbacks.

For instance, instead of writing "I wish I weren't so poor," you could write "I am financially independent." Alternatively, instead of "I wish I weren't constantly sad and upset," you may write, "I am pleased and capable of meeting obstacles with tolerance and impartiality."

Please keep it simple and as few words as possible. In other words, avoid becoming excessively verbose.

Too many words might be perplexing and detract from your concentration.

Third, picture and believe that the life you've imagined and constructed is genuinely yours because it is! All of our desires and goals begin in this manner; we cannot travel from point A to point B without first knowing addition; similarly, you cannot learn multiplication without first understanding addition.

Fourthly, you must have the ability to feel. How does it feel to be in the position you are in concerning your in-visioned goal?

See yourself fully immersed in your vision of a goal and that sensation, holding on to it as long as you can. Do this as much as possible until it becomes second nature. Until it's second nature to you and you bring it up without thinking.

Following that, you'll need to decide what you want to do. This is important for the start of your success. Write down five to ten activities that you appreciate on a spare piece of paper.

These do not have to be connected in any way. Following that, jot down the things you believe you are good at on the same sheet of paper. Take note of your strong points. Don't be hesitant to acknowledge your accomplishments! Recognize your achievements and abilities.

Then go back and re-read it until you get it. If you're stuck for ideas, it's okay. Before getting back to your project, take a break and do something completely unrelated. You will most likely have no issues.

Indeed, you may become overwhelmed by the number of ideas that come to mind; in that case, jot them down as quickly as they come to mind, and when you check your list, whatever jumps out the most is often your calling. You'll know based on your emotional reaction to it. Inspiration is confirmation that you are on the right track for developing your potential.

Allow yourself to be unnerved! The unknown IS frightening, and every entrepreneur can attest to this reality due to their personal experience. There is not a single successful person alive who has not experienced fear or intimidation at some point in their career.

The difference is that they overcame their fear; they ascended the ladder while others fell off one by one because they were terrified of the height.

Be willing to push yourself and overcome feelings of discomfort. When you want to transform your life and achieve financial freedom, you must change your behavior, and by doing this, you may encounter uncomfortable situations.

If you want to maintain your current comfort level, you must continue doing what you have been doing, but this also implies that you will not experience the change you so clearly desire.

To achieve the future and life you choose, you must make that intentional choice.

CHAPTER 8

Financial Planning For Individuals, Peace Of Mind And Freedom.

At some point, everyone has sought to improve their monthly income to pay off rising debts, whether through good personal financial planning or the assistance of an outside credit consulting organization.

Occasionally, the stress of restricted cash becomes too great to bear, and a strategy is considered necessary to establish financial freedom from creditors. Most consumers would be better suited to making their financial planning schedule. This activity entails full accountability and forces them to begin digging themselves out of a deep hole of debt.

To attain the financial freedom you've always desired, you must first integrate a personal financial planning system into your life and budget - and only then can you achieve economic serenity and freedom. Consider having no loans, no debts, and no mounting piles of bills - all of this is attainable if you establish a plan to get out of debt rather than talking about it.

1. Planning

Financial freedom is not difficult to accomplish; it only requires you to sit down and formulate an efficient hands-on approach to personal financial planning to erase your debts. Also, some experts recommend deactivating your credit cards to protect you from overspending. After all, if you lack the funds to purchase anything, you probably shouldn't.

Peace.

Even if you're drowning in debt, you can find some peace of mind. Millions of people in the United

States consult books and websites about the issue on a daily basis.

It's important to realize that you are not alone in your fight against debt; you can climb out of the hole and attain financial freedom with patience. Peace is gained when your financial planning blueprint is successfully implemented, but you cannot sit back and enjoy it; you must work for it.

Consider how credit card firms profit - by charging exorbitant interest and expecting you to pay only the bare minimum each month. Let's face it if you can't pay the minimum; then you should not be using or even having a credit card at this stage of life.

What can you do to get an advantage with such evident abuse of people's wallets?

Never pay only the minimum balance due but make all payments possible.

Avoid purchasing products that you do not require; preserve your money for a rainy day.

Change to a card that offers a cheaper interest rate or additional perks, rebates, or travel rewards.

Maintain a standard of living much below your salary; after all, there is no reason to brag.

Make prudent use of your credit card by creating a precise list of necessary expenses on your financial planning calendar.

Allow credit card firms to exploit you no longer - reclaim control of your financial circumstances and attain the financial freedom you desire. Paying off your obligations is the first step toward tranquility.

(2): Discard all credit cards except one that will be used for emergencies only. Keep this card out of your wallet, however.

Calculate your interest rates and total debt to get the exact monthly payment you want to make. Pay more than the minimum sum if you wish to avoid 30 years of debt but do the numbers. Make it a part of your financial planning calendar.

Prioritize paying off the credit card with the highest interest rate.

The most important thing to remember is to keep on track with your debt repayment plan and your overall financial goals. Conduct thorough research on your credit card terms - fees, charges, grace periods, and anything else you consider necessary. Spend the money you would have spent on credit firms on a better, more self-sufficient future after you have paid off all of your debts.

CONCLUSION.

Many people have worked very hard throughout their lives; however, they find themselves never able to attain their dreams of achieving financial freedom. Many people I know even sacrifice their personal or family time to make up that additional bit of success or money, yet they are still unsuccessful in attaining the goal.

Why? The answer is possible they have worked too hard! What?

Isn't it what our parents and teachers have always taught us from day one that you must work hard to earn a living and grow rich??!!

Financial Freedom defines a well-planned lifestyle where one no longer is compelled to labor for cash to support their costs." Being in a situation of financial freedom does not indicate that a person is required out of debt!

It means that one does not have to work for money anymore because money is working for one and is continuously more than enough to cover expenses, including debt. Ultimately, one can enjoy the chosen lifestyle without having to worry about money!

Some may argue, "How to earn money without having to work? That is impossible!" Indeed, it entails a significant shift in mentality. First, one must abandon the derogatory term "labor" and replace it with "system." For instance, franchising, network marketing. all these are systems.

Also, the term "system" is often used interchangeably with "automation." The point is to free oneself to focus on more value-added activities rather than being continually required to intervene directly in all large or minor concerns.

After you've grasped the concept of "Systems," you'll need to grasp the idea of "Leverage." Because a person's resources are restricted under their potential, it is important to understand how to LEVERAGE!

Have you gotten the picture? Once you've implemented a SYSTEM, the next thing you'll notice is constant cash flow generation. Network Marketing is an excellent sort of leveraging since you can successfully leverage all your downlines to support your business (and, of course, his own) and earn money for you anytime they earn money.

Although cash flow is often tiny at first, it grows with time owing to the compounding impact! Consider that you have five downlines in your network marketing organization and that each of those five people recruits another five people the following month.

Passive Income is the term popularly used to describe this type of cash flow generated systematically (or Residual Income). In essence, when one's passive income continually exceeds one's expenses, one is on the correct route toward financial freedom!

Stocks and real estate investments are also excellent sources of passive income—dividends from equities, rental income from real estate, etc. I'm aware of many wealthy individuals who get so much dividend income each year that they may effectively retire without having to worry about money.

Not to be forgotten is the Internet! The invention of the Internet has indeed created an enormous gateway for practically everyone on our planet to have a genuine opportunity to earn money without physically being there! Most significantly, the internet provides an ideal foundation for operating a 24-hour, seven-day-a-week money-making machine that never stops, even while you sleep!

Finally but certainly not least, a critical mindset shift is courage to take risks! Risk makes a person a better and more competitive person and it's what keeps a person's mind thinking more effectively to accomplish success! Leave your comfort zone in search of a more prosperous financial world!

Thanks for reading

Series: Financial Freedom at Any Age

1. Achieving Financial Freedom in your 20's
2. Achieving Financial Freedom in your 30's
3. Achieving Financial Freedom in your 40's
4. Achieving Financial Freedom in your 50's
5. Achieving Financial Freedom in your 60's
6. Achieving Financial Freedom in your 70's and beyond.
7. Achieving Financial Freedom in children
8. Achieving Financial Freedom in teenagers
9. Achieving Financial Freedom in college students.